www.finishinglinepress.com

Where Salt And Horses Live Without Man

poems by

Nina E. Larsen

Finishing Line Press
Georgetown, Kentucky

Where Salt And Horses Live Without Man

ACKNOWLEDGMENTS

"Dissecting Cod's Eye Day" was selected by Billy Collins for an honorable
mention in *The Fish Anthology 2012*
"The Horse" was selected by Leah Maines for *The Spirit of the Horse 2015.*
Indigo Rising Magazine (08/2011): "The Mermaid"

Publisher: Leah Maines

Editor: Christen Kincaid

Front Cover Art and Design: Christopher Haanes, http://christopherhaanes.com

Author Photo: Lumiere Photography, Singapore and Raul Escribano

Printed in the USA on acid-free paper.
Order online: www.finishinglinepress.com
also available on amazon.com

Author inquiries and mail orders:
Finishing Line Press
P. O. Box 1626
Georgetown, Kentucky 40324
U. S. A.

Table of Contents

For Linn Marie

Lofoten Islands

Born out of a tidal current,
  in the corner of the Northern Lights,

my father an ice breaker, my mother
  the early winter sun.

My twin sisters, icebergs,
  green and grey hypnotic moves,

my brothers, blue and pink
  winter mountains rising from deep fjords.

All gathered at the back of the North wind,
  I came out of the mouth of the morning sea.

I was followed by a wall of snow.
  A lynx walked me through it.

From the top of the polar circle,
  you can see me appearing for the first time,

a long, sandy beach dancing alone,
  where salt and horses live without man.

Dissecting Cod's Eye Day

A swallow, a whisper
from the time of the grandfathers,
diving outside.

A day you wake up early,
from the excitement of blood,
and the thought of intestines.

The good mood of all the boys,
the jumpiness of the girls.

Twelve tables covered with newspapers
and twelve cods.

We stand close,
the teacher holds the scalpel up in the air:
"Attention, here comes the scary moment!"
We behave well, angels in a circle.

The scalpel cuts carefully into the first eye,
a clean cut.
The teacher extracts the pearl of the eye:
a small lens, perfectly round; a jewel!

He rolls it gently on the newspaper,
we see the letters, enlarged one by one.
We travel through the crystal ball,

the discovery of a new world.
We bend our heads down,
looking through it from different angles,
the eye of the watcher is enlarged.

I see rings of light,
divine ships sailing out of bottles
into the night of candles,
my grandfather waving
from his little window;
a seagull eating
from his hand.

Tidal Wave

My father had the house bolted in four places,
his prayers built into a special construction
between the basement and the first floor.
Eddies growing under the streetlights on the road,
spinning closer with spin and speed,
they swallowed the background and the frame.
The wind against the walls, the windows moving,
we waited for the slinging of rock upon the bridge.
Then came the rain, and the flood,
water crashed through the house,
the rooms were soon knee deep in water,
I was placed on the fridge with a flashlight.

A snap close to me,
then another, a vibration, and the snap and the pop
in circular motion of the anchoring wires of the house
then a few seconds of silence,
the house moved, slowly moved and stopped.

The swish of the parachute rocket flare,
my father's face, a rainbow—
the triumph of an ark builder.

Dog Head

He told me he found a dog head
in the haunted house next door.

We entered the broken door,
in the corner, a broken skull.

The boy's blinking eyes,
in the dark, his wish became clear.

My skeptic eyebrow
counting the seconds of danger.

I took the coin from the ugly boy,
and showed him the difference between us,

I boxed a snail in his face,
walked out and showed him the fist of victory.

Migrants

I grew up as a stowaway
on gas tankers in the north Atlantic,
waving good bye to shadows,
I searched the ocean for signs to go on.
Birds always found me and saved me.
Arctic tern, oystercatchers and sea eagles,
taught me how to make my nest
in shafts and ventilation systems,
how to survive on cathedral[1] heat.
They treated me as their own and fed me
until I could take care of myself.

 I escaped my last ship.
Waves carried me; my roots grew sideways.
I travelled with an island of kelp.

I arrived at port at night,
the blurry lights burning.
The first steps on firm land,
wet stones everywhere,
wisdom of birds could not help.
I tried to stand up after falling,
embraced someone's leg,
reached for that stranger's hand.

[1]Cathedral is where the gas is kept on a gas tanker

Lion's Mane Jellyfish

Little lion is my hairstyle,
little devil is my style.

My fingers swim,
others sleep
in anemone forests.

Anywhere you
touch, I say yes
with burn marks.

There are
others who crave
my toxic legs.

I must go on
through ship propellers
to survive.

No fancy pearl from me,
but velvet dreams and
screams.

My jelly,
is my heart and my radar.

The Horse

Out of nowhere, came a horse,
the white horse followed the car all the way
on the bumpy forest road.
We drove as fast as we could,
but the small, old car
couldn't go faster than the horse.
I saw the horse in the back window,
furious, offended in some way.

I started throwing sugar cubes
out of the window.
The horse didn't care about them,
so we slowed down
worried that the horse,
would explode his heart.

The horse didn't stop,
he just continued running,
in the direction of the ferry,
as if he had more pre-historic reasons for running
and judging from those crazy eyes,
he was very late.

Puerto Escondido

After escaping Acapulco,
we ended up in a fishing village full of Italians
after some Cinema Paradiso man had done a movie
where a young man drinking Mescal and sleeping in a hammock,
found the meaning of life.
We tried it and we tried diving without a license,
the man said: You don't need one, you just need to go slowly down
not too deep, and so we did, my friend cured her fear of water
and we saw turtles and gold fish,
a killer whale from below,
and we were high on this diving experience,
just talking about turtles all day with the Italians,
joining a save the turtle association,
listening to Italian rock and drinking in hammocks,
until we had a ticket to go home
and we had our Latin exam where
Emperor Nero is looking out over Rome on fire
and we were there,
we burned of Italy and madness that summer,
we had warm, glowing faces from the fire
and flames in our mouth.

The Knife

The knife slipped out of my hand
and fell into the sea.
New on the boat, I tried to hide it,
I moved back to find a new knife.

As if my knife triggered a day of disaster,
our net was suddenly stuck in another boat's net.
Thousand meters of net entangled with
thousands of meters of rope.

The boats were drawn closer and closer,
the ugly noise of the engines,
but then the captain was waving with his knife,
it meant we had to cut.

All the fishermen were cutting and cutting,
me in the back pretending I was cutting,
feeling the captain's scowl on my back,
I kept my eyes on the water.

A silvery reflection of all of us,
melted with rainbows of oil spill,
a black cormorant drying his wings
on a cardinal mark.

Ropes and nets sunk and disappeared,
white shapes of dead fish, undersides of crabs,
we stood as in a funeral when suddenly
millions of tiny, green muted lights
rose up from the abyssal plain.

As if there is a God
in every little goodbye.

The Boat

I bought an old, wooden sailing boat;
it was a bad idea, like the Japanese whisky,
stalking loners from the islands,
lying about my past,
pretending I don't need glasses,
bringing a duck feather duvet onboard and candles,
cooking with white spirit onboard,
throwing the anchor into a car cemetery,
trying to start the old engine,
in front of champagne drinking men,
sails that got stuck and sent me the opposite way
and that boom boom boom, beating the breath out of me,
one two three, will my lungs ever come back—
a mink swimming away with my shoe.

Rock Awash

Already after the lighthouse,
something changed. No boats,
sniper rain, strange wind,
colors darker, waves deeper.

The sea started playing with our toy boat.
We; two Kabuki dolls, white,
stiff, balancing.

A dark shadow next to us, growing,
that grey coming,
it was a rock—

For some confusing seconds
we were wavering on top of the rock;
old shaky knife against old ironstone.

The wind sent us sideways,
then backwards down.
My friend's face, grey sculpture,

shocked to silence,
we were towed home
by smiling policemen.

We checked the chart
and there it was:
A tiny cross
with four dots in it;

a microscopic flag
from the unknown country,
that comes up to breathe,
twice a day:
rock awash, height unknown—

The small beautiful flooded palace

We were given yellow rubber boots at check in,
our suitcases placed in a rowing boat.
They told us we would get used to the smell,
by midnight the water would be gone.

We were given a key with a velvet tassel,
pure luxury, just holding that key,
we waded through the reception area,
given hot coffee with brandy in our room.

A small balcony, looking down on a canal,
a boat with wedding guests passed,
their good mood echoed between the buildings.
Our hands were cold, the yellow

made me realize it was all over.
The pleasures of the flooded palace,
jumped on to the passing boat and disappeared,
left us empty with a breakup to do.

The King Crab

The king crab eats everything:
Fish, kings, nets, hats,
wedding rings, oil tankers.
If you roll him a small stone
nothing comes out;
his rock mine digests all
with just a ticking sound,
water in water out,
crushing day and night,
the sideways walk.

Shafts of white crab meat,
waiting inside a shell tank,
hairy, spikey fingers, so fine but
impossible to break,
my hands sore from
scraping and pinching.

A sudden jump, to the open window,
his long legs escape
into the shadows of the places
where we used to hide.

The Boy from the Top of the Hill

Imagine one of those drawings from childhood
that take you from point to point,
from number to number.

From the milk moustaches of big brothers,
via buttons for an eye to the edge of black glasses
behind a newspaper,
the yellow house in the morning,
sitting in a blueberry bush,
my mother pointed up,
clues given by the play of shapes in the clouds,
birds eyes in the tree.
One glitter on top of a wave,
the one that looks a bit
like the end of a long summer,
and suddenly there he was
with a football in his piano hands,
my mother handing cake out of the window.
We ran down the rocky path
to see the new boats
coming in to paper boat harbor.

The cherry bonsai tree

It snowed outside when I entered the pool;
to a hotel spa in Japan by the sea,
in the corner a miniature garden, fresh and cool,
with moss, pine and a bonsai cherry tree.

Dreamlike appearing from a journey,
faeries lived there, cultivating their yin,
a small temple with the gardener Mr. Ishii,
I figure the cherries will have the size of a pin.

Will they land softly in the moss, I ask the tree?
The garden is meant to be relaxing only,
but I feel all sorts of worries, you see,
and who knows if the tree is lonely?

I must find a botanic expert insane and tough,
if flowers come, we must find a bee small enough.

The Mermaid

Just when you were leaving,
the sleeping candle woke up.
I started glowing in the dark,
but it was too late,
you were gone, you never got to know
about me being a mermaid
and how to know it is me,
when I come flapping my golden tail
against your old sailing boat
to sing for you.

The Spanish

I pulled a fish out of the water
bigger than you.
I cut his throat with a big knife,
I threw the gutter on the rocks,
it was my way of saying, I like you,
can you like me?
You took ten steps back and waited in the hills
with your watermelon.

I was a waving victory,
a lion eating on a zebra,
blood around my mouth.
You came down,
washed a drop of blood off my cheek
with your flowery shirt
and gave me a *beso*.

The watermelon made me forget,
the differences between us.
I threw the watermelon at you,
you ran away in slow motion.
It exploded when it landed,
on the rocks, red and green watermelon fiesta.
We got married soon after that.

The Little Girl God

"The Little Girl God" is the title of Marnie Weber's
art works at 100 Artists see God—a traveling exhibition
organized by ICI, New York 2004"

The Little Girl God took place in one of eleven rooms
of a large storybook dollhouse. In one room, we found a pearl
on the floor in a few drops of water, after the doll had risen
from the icy depths of a pond, to give a sermon
on finding God in simple things,
such as the laughter of a little girl.

The Forest

We watched as you let go
of the monk's leg,
the burgundy cotton safety net.
You walked on your toes,
stretched both hands up,
spread your fingers like fans,
waving to the two old pine trees—

as if you were older than us,
and knew that people who listen
to the wind in the pine trees
will travel back to the beginning
and all the images lived
from when we were born
will merge themselves with the forest,
and that moment
when we carried you home
through the spiraling rain
of ten thousand falling Huangshan pine umbrellas.

The Return

As simple as a child's drawing of a house,
blue and white, nestling on a rocky point,
stock fish drying on wooden racks,
his black bike in the doorway.

The man who used to scare me stiff
the way he lifted me up as a child,
hugging the breath out of me,
the rumbling laughter,
the smell of tobacco,
blueberry teeth.

He is on the docs,
walls of whale hanging on big hooks.
He is sawing on a wall of whale meat,
he is sawing a window,
he is standing in the middle,
laughing, waving to my daughter from a
window in the whale.

Nina E. Larsen is born in the Lofoten Islands of Norway. She has published work in Norway, the UK, Ireland and the US, been chosen by Billy Collins for an Honorable Mention in the 2012 Fish Poetry Prize. Recently published or forthcoming in *Narrative Northeast*, *The Spirit of the Horse: An Equine Anthology* (Finishing Line Press), and *20x20 Art Mag London*.

www.ingramcontent.com/pod-product-compliance
Lightning Source LLC
LaVergne TN
LVHW041330080426
835513LV00008B/662